AACHEN, GERMANY
TRAVEL GUIDE
2023-2024

The Best Travel Budget and Ultimate Travel Companion for Family Vacation, Lovers, Seniors, Tourists, Students and Solo Travelers

LISA HANSON

Copyright © 2023, Lisa Hanson

TABLE OF CONTENTS

CHAPTER THREE:

Exploring Aachen Neighborhoods

- Aachen's Historic Center
- Soers and the Sporting Spirit
- Vaals and International Vibes
- Grünes Dreieck: Aachen's Green Triangle

CHAPTER FOUR:

Must-See Attractions in Aachen

- Aachen Cathedral
- Carolus Thermen: Relaxation Oasis
- Aachener Tierpark: Zoo Adventure
- Ludwig Forum for Contemporary Art
- Couven Museum: Aachen's History in a Nutshell
- Dreiländereck: Three-Country Point

CHAPTER FIVE:

Savoring Aachen's Unique Culture

- Aachen's Culinary Delights
- Regional German Cuisine

APPENDIX III:

Maps of Aachen, Germany

INTRODUCTION

Welcome to the wonderful city of Aachen, Germany, dear travelers! As a witness to this city's awe-inspiring fabric of history, culture, and wonder, I am beyond happy to be your guide on this exhilarating adventure around Aachen in the years 2023-2024.

Imagine cobblestone alleys lined with lovely half-timbered cottages, a kaleidoscope of market booths bursting with tasty delights, and the enchanting chimes of the Aachen Cathedral bells vibrating through the air. This is Aachen, a city that seamlessly blends the past and present in a timeless dance.

In the pages of this travel guide, I will reveal the hidden gems and unforgettable experiences that await you in this medieval jewel of a city. Aachen boasts something extraordinary for every type of tourist, from the historic Charlemagne's Palatine Chapel, a UNESCO World Heritage Site, to the soothing waters of the Carolus Thermen spa, where you can wash your concerns away.

Explore the gastronomic center of Aachen, where the aroma of freshly baked Printen, a local specialty, wafts through the air. At rural taverns and Michelin-starred restaurants alike, savor the delicious flavors of traditional German food.

As you turn the pages of this guide, I'll take you on a fascinating tour through Aachen's rich history, from its reign as the capital of Charlemagne's empire to its modern-day importance as a center of innovation and academics. You'll be amazed by the stunning architecture, immersed in the pulsing energy of the city's vibrant festivals, and discovering the hidden pockets of tranquility that distinguish Aachen.

Aachen, however, is more than simply stone and history; it is a real, breathing entity with a flourishing arts and culture scene. Explore museums that house works by renowned painters, take in a spectacular play at the historic Theater Aachen, or simply meander around the city's bustling squares where street singers and artists weave their magic.

Prepare to be swept away by the Aachener people's warmth and hospitality. Their welcoming gestures and smiles will make you feel perfectly at home, leaving you with treasured memories to last a lifetime.

So, dear readers, whether you are an adventurous explorer, a history buff, a foodie, or simply a traveler seeking enchantment, Aachen invites you to embark on a memorable experience. Allow this "Aachen, Germany Travel Guide 2023-2024" to be your key to unlocking the doors of this enchanting city, where every turn unveils a new and captivating story.

I ask you to join me in experiencing the lovely city of Aachen, where history and modernity mingle to create a tapestry of amazement and wonder, as I share my amazing experiences and insider insights. Are you prepared to be enchanted by Aachen's magic? Turn the page to begin the journey!

CHAPTER ONE:
Introduction to Aachen

Discovering Aachen

Aachen, Germany, is a city in the heart of Europe that promises an exciting adventure to every visitor who passes its door. As you enter Aachen, you'll find yourself immersed in a mesmerizing blend of old-world beauty and modern vibrancy. It's a place where time seems to stand still as echoes of history echo down cobblestone streets, but it also pulses with the energy of a thriving, dynamic town.

Aachen is more than just a city; it's a treasure trove just waiting to be discovered. You'll find a rich tapestry of experiences here that cater to a wide range of interests. Whether you're a history buff wanting to follow in the footsteps of Charlemagne, a foodie eager to sample the distinct flavors of Printen and hearty German fare, or an art connoisseur looking for inspiration at world-class museums and galleries, Aachen has something special in store for you.

The warm surrounding of the city extends an open invitation to both single tourists seeking introspection and families seeking adventure. It's a place where you can easily interact with locals, who are famed for their warmth and friendliness, and who will make you feel like a valued guest in their community. The streets of Aachen are alive with activity, from bustling marketplaces to peaceful cafes where you may sip aromatic coffee while watching the world go by.

Brief History of Aachen

The history of Aachen is connected with Charlemagne's magnificence, who chose this city as the capital of his empire in the 9th century. The Palatine Chapel, Charlemagne's stately residence in Aachen, is a masterpiece of Carolingian architecture that still exists as a tribute to the strength and influence of this remarkable king.

Aachen became the focus of European politics and culture during Charlemagne's reign, attracting scholars, artists, and dignitaries from all across the continent.

With its beautiful mosaics and awe-inspiring grandeur, the city's Palatine Chapel, now a UNESCO World Heritage Site, remains a reminder of this golden age.

Aachen's importance persisted over the years, and the city's history is woven into its very fabric. Its cathedral, which features a remarkable blend of architectural styles ranging from Romanesque to Gothic, witnessed the crowning of countless German kings and emperors. Aachen is a living history book, with each cobblestone, structure, and square telling a story of perseverance and reinvention.

As you walk through Aachen's ancient streets and sites, you'll notice echoes of the past and the influence of Charlemagne's legacy, which continues to shape the city's identity today. The capacity of Aachen to perfectly mix its history with its lively present is what makes it a tempting destination for travelers seeking a unique blend of cultural richness and contemporary allure.

Geography and Climate

Aachen's geographical location adds yet another dimension to its allure. Situated in the western part of Germany, close to the borders of Belgium and the Netherlands, the city enjoys a strategic position that has influenced its history and culture. Surrounded by rolling hills and lush greenery, Aachen's natural beauty is as captivating as its architectural splendors.

The city's climate, while typically regarded as temperate, can be highly variable throughout the year. Summers are pleasant, with warm temperatures that allow exploring the city's outdoor attractions an enjoyable experience. The city's various parks and gardens, like the wonderfully maintained Kurpark, come alive with flowering flowers and picnickers, both locals and visitors.

Winters in Aachen, on the other hand, add a magical touch to the city. Snowfall blankets the cobblestone streets and antique buildings, transforming them into a stunning winter wonderland. The Aachen Christmas Market, one of Europe's most beautiful, lures visitors with its glittering lights, festive kiosks, and the smells of mulled wine and roasted chestnuts.

Getting to Aachen

Aachen is easy to reach because of its well-connected transportation network. If you're flying in from another country, you'll most likely land at Cologne Bonn Airport or Düsseldorf Airport, both of which provide easy access to Aachen. From there, you have several alternatives for transportation, including trains, buses, and rental automobiles.

The efficient German railway system, Deutsche Bahn, provides frequent connections to Aachen from major cities like Cologne, Brussels, and Amsterdam. The train journey itself is a scenic experience, offering picturesque views of the countryside as you approach Aachen's historic Hauptbahnhof (main train station).

Rental cars are widely accessible at airports for individuals who desire a more personalized experience. Driving to Aachen is a comfortable and convenient option because of Germany's well-maintained highways, which allow you to explore the city and its surrounding regions at your own speed.

Local Transportation

Once you've arrived in Aachen, getting around the city is a breeze, thanks to its efficient and reliable local transportation system. Aachen is known for its pedestrian-friendly streets, so exploring the city center on foot is a delightful option. The compact size of the city means that many of its attractions, restaurants, and shops are within easy walking distance of each other.

To travel further afield or explore the city's outskirts, there is a large network of buses and trams. The public transportation system in Aachen is not only convenient but also environmentally friendly, making it a good alternative for environmentally conscious travelers.

Bike rentals are widely accessible throughout the city for those who desire a little more independence. Aachen has a network of bike lanes and attractive cycling paths, making it an excellent opportunity to enjoy the city's charm while remaining active.

As we travel further into Aachen's heart in the pages ahead, you'll discover that the city's accessibility and transportation alternatives only contribute to its allure. So, ready to go on a trip that flawlessly blends history, culture, and convenience at this magnificent destination, dear reader. In the pages that follow, we'll take a journey through Aachen, where every turn exposes a new layer of its enthralling story. So, my reader, buckle in, because your adventure in Aachen has only just begun, and the delights of this city await your discovery.

CHAPTER TWO:
Planning Your Aachen Adventure

Choosing the Perfect Time to Visit

Aachen's attraction is not restricted to a single season; it shines all year, providing distinct pleasures in each. Let's look at the various charms of each season to help you design your ideal Aachen adventure:

1. Spring (March to May): Spring is a time of renewal in Aachen, with flowers blooming in the city's parks and gardens. The weather is good, making it excellent for outdoor activities. Temperatures will range from 8°C to 16°C (46°F to 61°F).

2. Summer (June to August): This is the busiest tourist season, with pleasant, sunny days. It's the great season for festivals, outdoor dining, and leisurely strolls, with temperatures ranging from 15°C to 24°C (59°F to 75°F).

3. Autumn (September to November): Aachen takes on a scenic appeal as the leaves change color. With temperatures ranging from 11°C to 20°C (52°F to 68°F), the weather stays pleasant. This is an excellent time to visit Aachen's cultural attractions.

4. Winter (December to February): Aachen transforms into a winter wonderland during the holiday season. The Christmas Market is a must-visit, and if you're lucky, you might even experience a snowy backdrop. Temperatures range from -1°C to 6°C (30°F to 43°F).

The best time to visit Aachen ultimately depends on your choices. Consider a winter visit if you enjoy festive atmospheres and pleasant experiences. Summer may be the season for you if you love warm weather and lively outside events.

Crafting Your Budget

Aachen has accommodations to suit all budgets. To help you manage your spending, here's a rough estimate:

- Budget Traveler (€50-€80 per day): Stay in hostels or budget guesthouses, enjoy street food and local eateries, and use public transportation. This budget is ideal for frugal travelers who want to experience Aachen without breaking the bank.

- Mid-Range Traveler (€80-€150 per day): Choose from cozy three-star hotels or beautiful bed-and-breakfasts. Explore more sites and activities while enjoying a variety of dining experiences ranging from local cafés to mid-range restaurants.

- Luxury Traveler (€150+ per day): Indulge in five-star lodgings, exquisite dining, and private tours. This budget guarantees an opulent and unique Aachen experience.

Accommodation Options

1. Dorint Hotel Aachen (Luxury)
   - Address: Peterstraße 66, 52062 Aachen, Germany
   - Contact: Phone: +49 241 18010
   - Website: www.dorint.com/aachen

2. INNSIDE Aachen (Mid-Range)

- Address: Sandkaulstraße 20, 52062 Aachen, Germany

- Contact: Phone: +49 241 18040

-Website: www.melia.com/en/hotels/germany/aachen/innside-aachen

3. A&O Aachen Hauptbahnhof (Budget)

- Address: Hackländerstraße 5, 52064 Aachen, Germany

- Contact: Phone: +49 241 4502380

- Website: www.aohostels.com/en/aachen/aachen-hauptbahnhof

4. Gästehaus Aachen (Budget)

- Address: Reumontstraße 29, 52064 Aachen, Germany

- Contact: Phone: +49 241 4003981

- Website: www.gaestehaus-aachen.de/en

These accommodation options cater to various budgets and preferences. Be sure to book in advance, especially during the peak tourist season, to secure your stay in this enchanting city.

Crafting Your Itinerary

Now that you've chosen the perfect time to visit, considered your budget, and selected your accommodation, it's time to create an itinerary that will allow you to make the most of your Aachen adventure. Here's a thrilling and diverse sample itinerary to ignite your wanderlust:

Day 1: Arrival and Aachen's Historic Core
- Morning: Arrive in Aachen and settle into your chosen accommodation.

- Afternoon: Begin your journey in Aachen's historic core. Explore the Aachen Cathedral (Dom), marveling at its awe-inspiring architecture and the Palatine Chapel within. Don't miss Charlemagne's Palatine Chapel, a true masterpiece.

- Evening: Stroll through the lively streets around the cathedral, where you'll find an array of charming cafes and restaurants for a delightful dinner.

Day 2: Cultural Immersion

- Morning: Start your day at the Centre Charlemagne, an interactive museum that delves into Aachen's history. Learn about Charlemagne's legacy and the city's evolution.

- Afternoon: Visit the Suermondt-Ludwig-Museum, where you can admire an impressive collection of European art spanning centuries.

- Evening: Immerse yourself in Aachen's vibrant culture by attending a performance at Theater Aachen or catching live music at a local venue.

Day 3: Culinary Delights

- Morning: Begin your day with a visit to the Aachen Market, where local vendors sell fresh produce, cheeses, and crafts. Savor a delightful breakfast at one of the market's food stalls.

- Afternoon: Take a short trip to the Lindt Chocolate Factory Outlet, just outside Aachen, and indulge in some of the finest Swiss chocolates.

- Evening: Satisfy your taste buds with traditional German cuisine at a local tavern. Don't forget to try the local specialty, Printen, a spiced gingerbread cookie.

Day 4: Natural Beauty and Relaxation

- Morning: Spend your morning in the Aachener Wald, a serene forested area just outside the city. Explore its walking trails and take in the fresh air.

- Afternoon: Pamper yourself at the Carolus Thermen spa, where you can relax in thermal baths, saunas, and wellness facilities.

- Evening: Savor a leisurely dinner at one of Aachen's upscale restaurants, indulging in exquisite cuisine.

Day 5: Exploring Beyond Aachen

- Morning: Take a day trip to the picturesque town of Monschau, known for its well-preserved half-timbered houses. Explore the town center and enjoy a traditional German lunch.

- Afternoon: Visit the Eifel National Park, where you can hike through pristine natural landscapes and soak in the beauty of the region.

- Evening: Return to Aachen and have dinner at a cozy restaurant, reminiscing about your day of adventure.

Travel Essentials and Packing Hints

1. Comfortable Walking Shoes: Aachen's charm lies in its walkable streets, so bring comfortable shoes for exploring the city.

2. Weather-appropriate Clothing: Bring layers to account for Aachen's changing weather. Bring a raincoat or umbrella, especially if you're visiting in the spring or autumn.

3. Power Adapter: Germany uses the European two-pin plug type (Type C and Type F), so ensure you have the right adapter for your devices.

4. Travel Guidebook: While this guide provides valuable insights, consider bringing a physical or digital travel guidebook for on-the-go reference.

5. Language Essentials: While many people speak English, knowing a few German phrases can enhance your experience. As such, I provide some basic and useful German phrases to help you at the appendix of this guide.

6. Reusable Water Bottle: Keep hydrated while exploring Aachen. Many establishments provide free tap water refills.

7. Camera or Smartphone: Use your camera or smartphone to capture the beauty of Aachen and create memorable memories.

8. Travel Insurance: Having travel insurance to cover unexpected situations during your travels is usually a good idea.

9. Local Currency: Bring some euros in cash for little purchases, as not all establishments take credit cards.

10. Daypack: A tiny daypack is useful for carrying essentials while exploring Aachen.

With your itinerary carefully crafted and your travel essentials packed, you're well-prepared for an exciting and immersive adventure in Aachen. Get ready to uncover the magic of this remarkable city, where every day brings new discoveries and unforgettable experiences. As you plan your adventure in Aachen, consider the season that aligns with your interests and budget. With the right timing and accommodations, you'll be well-prepared to immerse yourself in the magic of Aachen, where history and modernity converge in a symphony of experiences.

CHAPTER THREE:
Exploring Aachen Neighborhoods

Aachen's Historic Center

The historic center of Aachen is the city's heart and soul, where the past and present collide in a captivating blend of architecture, culture, and lively vitality. The Aachen Cathedral, a UNESCO World Heritage Site, and Charlemagne's Palatine Chapel are at its heart. These historic structures exude a timeless grandeur, with breathtaking interiors embellished with elaborate mosaics and priceless treasures.

Wander through the cobblestone streets, and you'll discover charming boutiques, inviting cafes, and bustling marketplaces. The Elisenbrunnen, a neo-classical pavilion, is a favorite spot for locals and visitors alike to relax and sip the city's famous healing waters. As you explore this neighborhood, you'll feel like you're stepping into a living history book, where each building and corner tells a tale of Aachen's rich heritage.

Soers and the Sporting Spirit

Soers is the neighborhood to visit if you have a passion for sports and a taste for adventure. The Aachen-Laurensberger Rennverein (ALRV), one of Europe's most prominent equestrian centers, is located in this area. The CHIO Aachen World Equestrian Festival attracts viewers every July with thrilling showjumping, dressage, and driving competitions.

The Tivoli Stadium, adjacent to the equestrian grounds, is where football fans can watch Alemannia Aachen play. The sporting zeal here is contagious, and even if you're not a sports fan, the electric atmosphere and camaraderie will leave an indelible impact.

Vaals and International Vibes

Crossing the border into the Netherlands, just a short drive from Aachen, you'll find the charming town of Vaals. This international enclave offers a delightful change of scenery and culture. One of its main attractions is the Vaalsberg, the highest point in the Netherlands, where you can stand in three countries at once – Germany, the Netherlands, and Belgium.

Visit Drielandenpunt, a monument commemorating this unusual meeting point from which you may enjoy panoramic views of the surrounding landscape. Vaals also has a vibrant market square and a variety of pleasant cafes and restaurants, making it an ideal day excursion to experience international vibes without leaving Aachen.

Grünes Dreieck: Aachen's Green Triangle

Nature enthusiasts and those seeking tranquility will find solace in Grünes Dreieck, Aachen's Green Triangle. This lush and verdant neighborhood offers a peaceful escape from the bustling city center. Explore the Aachener Wald, a vast forested area with hiking and biking trails that wind through ancient trees and serene ponds.

Another gem in this area is the Lousberg, a hill crowned with an observation tower offering breathtaking views of Aachen. The Lousberg is an ideal spot for picnics, contemplation, or simply enjoying the fresh air. As you wander through this neighborhood, you'll discover a harmonious balance between urban life and natural beauty, making it a tranquil oasis within Aachen's boundaries.

From digging into the city's history in the historic center to embracing the sporting spirit in Soers, experiencing international vibes in Vaals, and finding serenity in the Green Triangle, each of these Aachen neighborhoods offers a unique and engaging experience. Aachen has a neighborhood for everyone, no matter what your interests are.

CHAPTER FOUR:
Must-See Attractions in Aachen

Aachen Cathedral

At the heart of Aachen's historic center stands the awe-inspiring Aachen Cathedral, locally known as the "Dom." This architectural masterpiece is a testament to the city's rich history and religious significance. Its construction began in the 8th century under the patronage of Charlemagne, and it served as the imperial palace chapel for centuries.

The beautiful Palatine Chapel, a UNESCO World Heritage Site, greets you as you enter the church. Admire the exquisite mosaics and golden chandelier that illuminate this hallowed sanctuary in a hypnotic play of light and color. The shrine to Charlemagne, which houses his relics, contributes to the eerie atmosphere.

Climb the octagonal tower of the Palatine Chapel for panoramic views of the city, where you can see the cobblestone streets and old buildings below. A visit to the Aachen Cathedral is a voyage through time and religion, and it is an absolute must-see for anybody visiting this beautiful city.

Aachen Cathedral

Carolus Thermen: Relaxation Oasis

Carolus Thermen is a calm retreat away from the rush and bustle of the city. This thermal spa complex, located near Aachen's historic center, provides a haven of relaxation and regeneration. Carolus Thermen's curative waters have been sought after for generations, and visitors can now immerse themselves in thermal baths, saunas, and wellness treatments.

Indulge in the warm, mineral-rich waters, which are reputed to have medicinal characteristics, or relax in the scented saunas, each with its own theme and atmosphere. The outdoor pools are exceptionally lovely, surrounded by lush foliage and providing pleasant relaxation all year.

Whether you're seeking a romantic escape, a solo retreat, or a family day of relaxation, Carolus Thermen provides an oasis of serenity in the heart of Aachen.

Carolus Thermen

Aachener Tierpark: Zoo Adventure

Aachener Tierpark is a must-see site for animal lovers and families. This quaint zoo houses a diverse array of animals from all over the world, making it a fun adventure for visitors of all ages.

Stroll through beautifully landscaped enclosures and observe exotic species, including playful lemurs, majestic big cats, and colorful birds. The zoo's emphasis on conservation and education ensures a meaningful experience, as you learn about the natural habitats and behaviors of the animals.

Aachener Tierpark's dedication to animal welfare and its interactive exhibits, such as the petting zoo, make it a wonderful place to connect with the animal kingdom and foster a sense of wonder and appreciation for wildlife.

Aachener Tierpark

Ludwig Forum for Contemporary Art

For art enthusiasts, the Ludwig Forum for Contemporary Art is a haven of creativity and innovation. Housed in a striking glass building that contrasts with Aachen's historic architecture, this museum showcases contemporary art in all its forms.

Explore thought-provoking exhibitions presenting renowned artists' works, ranging from modern paintings and sculptures to multimedia installations and avant-garde pieces. The museum's constantly changing exhibits ensure that each visit is a new and exciting experience.

The Ludwig Forum also hosts cultural events, workshops, and lectures, allowing visitors to interact with the art community and get insight into the ever-changing world of contemporary art. It's a location where creativity has no limits and where you can immerse yourself in Aachen's cutting-edge art scene.

Ludwig Forum

Couven Museum: Aachen's History in a Nutshell

To delve deeper into Aachen's rich history, a visit to the Couven Museum is a must. This charming museum, housed in a historic townhouse, offers a glimpse into the daily life and culture of Aachen over the centuries.

Explore beautifully restored historical rooms decorated with real furniture, decor, and artifacts. Discover exhibits ranging from traditional handcraft to the history of Aachen's architecture. The museum's collection depicts Aachen's transformation from a medieval hamlet to a flourishing city.

The Couven Museum offers an intriguing glimpse into the past, allowing you to travel back in time and better comprehend the city's cultural legacy and character.

Couven Museum, Aachen

Dreiländereck: Three-Country Point

Travel to the boundaries of Germany, the Netherlands, and Belgium to find the Dreiländereck, or Three-Country Point. This one-of-a-kind geographical location is recognized by a monument that permits you to stand in three nations at the same time.

Enjoy panoramic views of the surrounding countryside from the monument's platform, and take memorable photos as you straddle the borders. The Dreiländereck is a symbol of unity and cooperation in the heart of Europe, and it's a testament to the region's rich history and cultural diversity.

Pack a picnic and spend a leisurely afternoon in this tranquil setting, pondering the significance of this meeting point and the shared history of these neighboring countries. It's a testament to Aachen's international appeal and its role as a crossroads of cultures and histories.

Dreiländereck

From exploring the city's spiritual heart at the Aachen Cathedral to finding relaxation at Carolus Thermen, going on a zoo adventure at Aachener Tierpark, immersing yourself in contemporary art at the Ludwig Forum, delving into Aachen's history at the Couven Museum, and standing at the crossroads of nations at

Dreiländereck, each of these must-see attractions in Aachen offers a unique and enriching experience. Your journey around Aachen will be a stunning tapestry of memorable moments.

CHAPTER FIVE:

Savoring Aachen's Unique Culture

Aachen's Culinary Delights

Aachen's culinary scene is a delightful fusion of tradition and innovation, offering a gastronomic journey like no other. Start your culinary adventure with a taste of the city's most famous treat, Printen. These spiced gingerbread cookies are an Aachen specialty and can be found in various forms, from traditional to chocolate-coated and even liqueur-filled.

For savory delights, explore the city's lively marketplaces, where local vendors offer fresh produce, cheeses, sausages, and more. Don't miss the chance to try "Aachener Sauerbraten," a regional pot roast dish, or "Himmel und Äad," a comforting combination of mashed potatoes and apples.

Aachen's cafe culture is also a must-experience. Sip a cup of aromatic coffee at a local cafe while savoring a slice of "Streuselkuchen" (crumb cake) or a "Kirschplunder" (cherry pastry). The cafes here are not just places to eat and drink; they are cultural hubs where locals gather to socialize and enjoy the simple pleasures of life.

Regional German Cuisine

While in Aachen, take the opportunity to explore the rich tapestry of German cuisine. Sample traditional dishes like "Rouladen" (beef rolls), "Kartoffelsalat" (potato salad), and "Bratwurst" (sausages) prepared with local flair. Pair your meal with a glass of "Kölsch," a regional beer from nearby Cologne, or indulge in some "Apfelwein," a German apple wine.

If you're feeling adventurous, delve into "Eifeler Döppekuchen," a hearty potato casserole that's a regional favorite. Aachen's proximity to the Netherlands and Belgium also means you can savor Flemish influences, such as "Carbonade flamande" (a beer-based beef stew) and "Moules-frites" (mussels with fries).

For dessert, explore the world of German pastries and cakes. Indulge in a slice of "Schwarzwälder Kirschtorte" (Black Forest cake) or "Apfelstrudel" (apple strudel) while sipping on a cup of herbal tea or a glass of fine German wine.

Festivals and Cultural Events

Aachen's calendar is punctuated by a lively array of festivals and cultural events that showcase the city's vibrant spirit. One of the highlights is the Aachen Christmas Market, a magical extravaganza that transforms the city center into a winter wonderland. Stroll through the market's charming stalls, savoring mulled wine, roasted chestnuts, and other festive treats.

The CHIO Aachen World Equestrian Festival, held every July, is another grand event that captivates locals and visitors alike. This equestrian competition brings together riders from around the world to showcase their skills in showjumping, dressage, and driving. The atmosphere is electric, with a mix of sporting excitement and social gatherings.

Throughout the year, Aachen hosts cultural festivals, including music performances, art exhibitions, and theater productions. Be sure to check the local event calendar to coincide your visit with these enriching cultural experiences.

Performing Arts and Local Theater

Aachen boasts a thriving performing arts scene, with theaters and venues that offer a diverse range of cultural performances. Theater Aachen, in particular, is a hub of creativity and entertainment. Attend a ballet, opera, or drama performance in this historic theater, which has been a cultural cornerstone of the city for centuries.

The city also features smaller theaters and stages that showcase local talent and emerging artists. These intimate venues offer a more personal and immersive theater experience, allowing you to connect with the local arts community.

Whether you're a fan of classical music, contemporary dance, or thought-provoking theater, Aachen's performing arts scene has something to offer every cultural enthusiast.

Arts and Crafts of Aachen

Aachen's rich artistic heritage extends beyond the realm of culinary delights and theater. The city has a thriving arts and crafts community, where talented artisans produce exquisite handcrafted goods.

Explore local markets and artisan workshops to discover unique items such as hand-blown glassware, ceramics, jewelry, and textiles. Aachen is known for its tradition of craftsmanship, and many of these artisans draw inspiration from the city's rich history and cultural diversity.

You can also visit the Arts and Crafts Market in the historic center to witness the creative process firsthand and purchase one-of-a-kind souvenirs that embody Aachen's unique culture.

In Aachen, culture is not merely a facet of life; it's a way of life. From savoring culinary delights and embracing regional German cuisine to participating in lively festivals, immersing yourself in the performing arts, and exploring the craftsmanship of the city, Aachen's culture is a vibrant tapestry that invites you to savor every moment of your visit.

CHAPTER SIX:
Outdoor Adventures and Recreation

Parks and Green Spaces

Aachen offers a plethora of parks and green spaces that invite both locals and visitors to bask in the beauty of nature. Among the most beloved is the Elisenbrunnen Park, an oasis of tranquility nestled in the heart of the city. Here, you can stroll through lush gardens, relax by the tranquil fountains, and take in the fresh air as you admire the neoclassical architecture of the Elisenbrunnen pavilion.

For a more extensive natural escape, the Aachener Wald (Aachen Forest) awaits just outside the city. This expansive forested area offers a network of hiking trails, perfect for nature enthusiasts. Picnic spots, meandering streams, and peaceful groves make it an ideal destination for a day in the great outdoors.

Biking in the Eifel Region

Aachen is a gateway to the stunning Eifel region, renowned for its picturesque landscapes and extensive network of cycling trails. Grab a bike and explore the rolling hills, dense forests, and serene lakes of this remarkable region. The Vennbahn Radweg, a former railway line turned cycling path, offers a scenic route through the Eifel, taking you past charming villages and historical landmarks.

Whether you're an avid cyclist or a leisurely rider, the Eifel region provides an array of biking experiences to suit all levels of expertise. Bike rentals are readily available in Aachen, making it easy to embark on your two-wheeled adventure.

Hiking in the Hautes Fagnes

For those seeking an exhilarating hiking experience, the nearby Hautes Fagnes (High Fens) nature reserve beckons with its wild and rugged beauty. This vast moorland, located on the Belgian-German border, offers a diverse range of hiking trails that wind through wetlands, forests, and open plateaus.

One of the most captivating trails is the Fagnes-Hohes Venn trail, which meanders through this unique landscape, passing by pristine peat bogs, picturesque lakes, and an abundance of flora and fauna. It's an opportunity to immerse yourself in nature and discover the enchanting ecosystems of the Hautes Fagnes.

Water Activities on the Wurm River

The Wurm River, which flows through Aachen, provides opportunities for water-based activities and leisurely moments by the water's edge. You can rent a kayak or canoe and paddle along the scenic stretches of the Wurm, allowing you to observe the city from a different perspective.

The riverbanks also make for perfect picnic spots and leisurely walks, offering a peaceful escape from the urban hustle and bustle. For those who prefer a more relaxed experience, simply find a serene spot to sit and enjoy the soothing sounds of the flowing water.

Golfing in Aachen

Golf enthusiasts will find several well-maintained golf courses in and around Aachen. The city's golf clubs provide an opportunity to tee off in beautiful surroundings while enjoying the fresh air and green landscapes.

One of the prominent golf clubs in the region is the Aachener Golf-Club 1927 e.V., which boasts an 18-hole course set against the backdrop of the scenic Eifel hills. Whether you're a seasoned golfer or a beginner, these courses offer an enjoyable day on the greens.

Day Trips to Maastricht and Cologne

Aachen's strategic location makes it an ideal starting point for exciting day trips to neighboring cities. Just a short drive away is Maastricht, a charming Dutch city known for its historic architecture, vibrant cultural scene, and delectable cuisine. Explore its cobbled streets, visit the renowned Bonnefanten Museum, and savor Dutch treats in cozy cafes.

Another excellent day trip option is Cologne, home to the iconic Cologne Cathedral (Kölner Dom), a UNESCO World Heritage Site. Discover the city's rich history, explore the bustling Cologne Old Town, and take a stroll along the Rhine River promenade. Cologne is also famous for its carnival celebrations and vibrant festivals throughout the year.

Whether you choose to immerse yourself in nature's beauty, indulge in outdoor activities, or embark on cultural day trips, Aachen offers a wealth of outdoor adventures and recreational opportunities that cater to all interests and preferences. Each experience promises a unique way to enjoy the breathtaking landscapes and rich culture of this captivating region.

CHAPTER SEVEN:
Aachen for Every Traveler

Ladies and gentlemen, as a witness to the splendors of Aachen, I am honored to present Chapter 7, where I share my firsthand experience of Aachen's unique appeal to travelers of all ages, interests, and circumstances. Aachen, you see, is a city that welcomes every kind of adventurer with open arms.

Family-Friendly Activities

For families, Aachen is a treasure trove of enriching experiences. The Aachener Tierpark is a wonderful place for kids to encounter diverse wildlife, while the Ludwig Forum's interactive exhibitions ignite the imaginations of young and old alike. Don't forget to indulge in a Printen-making workshop, where little hands can create delicious gingerbread cookies to savor later.

Exploring Aachen's parks, such as the Elisenbrunnen Park and the Aachener Wald, provides excellent opportunities for outdoor family fun. The nearby Eifel region offers exciting hiking trails, picnics by pristine lakes, and the chance to embark on family bike rides through beautiful landscapes.

Romantic Escapes for Lovers

Aachen's romantic ambiance casts a spell on lovers seeking a romantic escape. Begin your day with a leisurely breakfast at one of the city's charming cafes, where you can savor coffee and pastries while gazing into each other's eyes.

Stroll hand in hand through the historic center, marveling at the Aachen Cathedral's intricate architecture and basking in the serenity of Elisenbrunnen Park. As the evening sets in, dine in cozy restaurants offering candle lit dinners and intimate settings.

Carolus Thermen beckons for a relaxing day of unwinding together. The soothing thermal baths and saunas provide a perfect backdrop for couples to bond and rejuvenate. Finally, why not take a day trip to the romantic city of Maastricht, just a short drive away, where you can explore quaint streets, dine along picturesque canals, and create memories together.

Aachen for Seniors

Aachen is a city where seniors can explore its rich history and culture at a leisurely pace. The Couven

Museum offers a glimpse into Aachen's past, and the Aachen Cathedral welcomes visitors of all ages to marvel at its beauty. Accessible walking paths and well-maintained gardens make it easy for seniors to explore the city's historic core.

Aachener Tierpark, with its relaxed ambiance, is an ideal destination for senior travelers who enjoy observing animals and spending time outdoors. The city's public transportation system is efficient and accessible, ensuring seniors can navigate Aachen with ease.

Aachen for Students

For students, Aachen offers a vibrant mix of culture, history, and youthful energy. Join in the lively atmosphere of Aachen's many festivals and cultural events, such as the Aachen Christmas Market and the CHIO Aachen World Equestrian Festival.

Aachen's university town spirit means there are plenty of budget-friendly eateries and bars where students can savor local cuisine and meet fellow travelers. Explore the city's nightlife, where you can dance the night away or enjoy live music performances at local venues.

The city's proximity to the Eifel region provides opportunities for students to partake in outdoor adventures, from hiking and biking to kayaking on the Wurm River. And when it's time for a break, consider a day trip to vibrant Cologne for a dose of urban excitement.

Solo Travel Tips and Safety

Solo travelers, fear not! Aachen is a safe and welcoming city for those exploring on their own. Start your journey with a guided city tour to get your bearings and learn about the city's history and culture. The Aachen Cathedral's serene interior is an excellent place for reflection and contemplation.

Aachen's compact size and pedestrian-friendly streets make it easy to navigate, and the city's friendly locals are always ready to offer assistance or strike up a conversation. To enhance safety, stick to well-lit areas at night and keep your belongings secure.

Solo travelers can take advantage of the city's cultural events, museums, and cafes to meet fellow explorers and make new friends. Don't hesitate to join a local group or tour if you'd like some company while discovering the wonders of Aachen.

So, whether you're a family looking for memorable moments, a couple seeking a romantic getaway, a senior traveler embracing history, a student exploring culture, or a solo adventurer savoring freedom, Aachen beckons with a warm embrace and endless possibilities. In Aachen, there's a place for everyone, and each journey is destined to be unforgettable.

CHAPTER EIGHT: Practical Information and Resources

Money Matters and Currency Exchange

Before setting off on your Aachen adventure, it's important to be familiar with the local currency and banking system. Germany uses the euro (€) as its official currency. ATMs are readily available throughout the city, allowing you to withdraw euros as needed. Credit cards are widely accepted, but it's advisable to carry some cash for smaller expenses and in case you encounter places that do not accept cards.

Currency exchange services are available at banks and exchange offices, although exchange rates may vary. Be sure to check with your bank for any international transaction fees associated with using your credit or debit card abroad.

Language and Communication

German is the official language in Aachen, but English is widely spoken, especially in tourist areas and among the younger population. Most signs and information are also provided in English, making it convenient for travelers who may not be fluent in German.

To enhance your travel experience, consider learning a few basic German phrases. Locals often appreciate when visitors make an effort to speak their language, even if it's just a simple "Danke" (thank you) or "Guten Tag" (good day).

For staying connected, mobile phone coverage is excellent in Aachen, and you can easily purchase a prepaid SIM card with data for your smartphone. Free Wi-Fi is available at many hotels, cafes, and public spaces.

Staying Safe and Healthy

Aachen is generally a safe city for travelers. However, it's always wise to take precautions to ensure your safety and well-being. Here are some tips:

- Emergency Services: In case of an emergency, dial 112 for immediate assistance. Aachen has a well-trained emergency response system.

- Healthcare: Aachen boasts a high standard of healthcare facilities. The city has hospitals, clinics, and pharmacies where you can receive medical assistance if needed. It's advisable to have travel insurance that covers medical emergencies.

- Safety: Aachen is a safe city to explore, but it's important to exercise the same caution you would in any urban area. Keep an eye on your belongings, especially in crowded places, and be aware of your surroundings, particularly at night.

- Weather: Be prepared for varying weather conditions, as Aachen experiences all four seasons. Dress appropriately and check the weather forecast before heading out.

- Travel Insurance: Consider purchasing travel insurance that covers unexpected events, such as trip cancellations, lost luggage, and medical emergencies. It provides peace of mind and ensures you're protected during your journey.

- Vaccinations: Check with your healthcare provider regarding any recommended vaccinations or health precautions before traveling to Aachen.

- Local Laws and Customs: Familiarize yourself with local laws and customs, including rules related to smoking, alcohol consumption, and public behavior.

- Emergency Contacts: Keep a list of important phone numbers, including your country's embassy or consulate in Germany, as well as contact information for your accommodations.

Sustainable Travel in Aachen

As responsible travelers, it's essential to consider the impact of our journeys on the environment and local communities. Aachen encourages sustainable tourism practices, and there are several ways you can contribute to eco-friendly travel while exploring this beautiful city:

1. Public Transportation: Aachen has an efficient and well-connected public transportation system, including buses and trams. Opt for public transport whenever possible to reduce your carbon footprint.

2. Walking and Biking: Aachen is a pedestrian-friendly city with dedicated bike lanes. Explore the city center on foot or rent a bicycle to experience Aachen at a leisurely pace while minimizing emissions.

3. Reduce, Reuse, Recycle: Be mindful of your waste disposal. Many public spaces in Aachen have recycling bins for paper, plastic, and glass. Reduce single-use plastics by carrying a reusable water bottle and shopping bag.

4. Eco-Friendly Accommodations: Consider staying in eco-friendly accommodations that prioritize sustainability and responsible tourism practices. Look for hotels or guesthouses with green certifications.

5. Support Local and Sustainable Dining: Choose restaurants and eateries that emphasize locally sourced and seasonal ingredients. By enjoying regional cuisine, you support local farmers and reduce food miles.

6. Respect Nature and Wildlife: If you venture into Aachen's natural areas, such as the Aachener Wald or the Hautes Fagnes, be sure to follow Leave No Trace principles, respecting the flora and fauna, and staying on designated trails.

7. Shop Responsibly: When purchasing souvenirs or gifts, opt for items that are locally made or crafted using sustainable materials. Avoid buying products

made from endangered species or contributing to illegal wildlife trade.

By adopting these sustainable practices, you can minimize your environmental impact while making a positive contribution to the well-being of Aachen and its surroundings.

Essential Contacts and Emergency Numbers

When traveling to Aachen, it's crucial to have access to essential contacts and emergency numbers. Here are some updated samples of contact information you should keep handy:

- Emergency Services: Dial 112 for emergency assistance, including police, fire, medical, and other emergencies. This number is available throughout Europe.

- Local Police: For non-emergency matters and general inquiries, you can contact the local police at the Aachen Police Department:
  - Aachen Police Department
  - Address: Kaiserplatz 2, 52064 Aachen, Germany
  - Phone: +49 241 95770

- Medical Assistance: In case of a medical emergency, you can reach out to the University Hospital RWTH Aachen (Universitätsklinikum Aachen):
  - University Hospital RWTH Aachen
  - Address: Pauwelsstraße 30, 52074 Aachen, Germany
  - Phone: +49 241 80-0

- Lost or Stolen Passport: If you are a foreign traveler and your passport is lost or stolen, contact your country's embassy or consulate. Here's the contact information for the U.S. Embassy in Berlin:

- U.S. Embassy Berlin
- Address: Pariser Platz 2, 10117 Berlin, Germany
- Phone: +49 30 83050

- Local Tourist Information: For tourist information, maps, and assistance, you can visit the Aachen Tourist Service Center:
  - Aachen Tourist Service Center
  - Address: Markt 45, 52062 Aachen, Germany
  - Phone: +49 241 1802960

- Currency Exchange: In Aachen, you can exchange currency at various banks, exchange offices, and even at the train station. Consider contacting your bank for information on currency exchange rates and fees.

- Transportation Services: For information on public transportation, including schedules and routes, you can contact ASEAG (Aachener Straßenbahn und

Energieversorgungs-AG), Aachen's public transport company:

 - ASEAG
 - Address: Lütticher Str. 10, 52064 Aachen, Germany
 - Phone: +49 241 1688-0

Having these essential contacts and emergency numbers readily available can provide you with peace of mind during your visit to Aachen, ensuring that you can access assistance or information when needed. With these practical details at your fingertips, you are well-prepared to embark on your Aachen journey. May your time in this enchanting city be filled with discovery, adventure, and unforgettable memories. Safe travels!

APPENDIX I:
Useful Travel Resources

As you prepare for your journey to Aachen, these travel resources will prove invaluable in ensuring a smooth and enjoyable experience.

Handy Travel Apps

1. Google Maps: Navigate the city with ease, find nearby attractions, and access public transportation information.

2. Duolingo: Brush up on your German language skills with this user-friendly language learning app.

3. XE Currency: Stay updated on currency exchange rates, making it easier to manage your finances while abroad.

4. Aachen City Guide: Download this app for detailed information on Aachen's attractions, restaurants, and events.

5. TripAdvisor: Use this app to read reviews and recommendations from fellow travelers about hotels, restaurants, and attractions in Aachen.

6. DB Navigator: If you plan on exploring Germany by train, this app provides schedules, ticket booking, and platform information for Deutsche Bahn trains.

7. Weather Apps: Check weather conditions in Aachen before your daily adventures. Popular options include

Weather.com, AccuWeather, or your smartphone's built-in weather app.

Aachen Travel Checklist

Before departing for Aachen, make sure to review this checklist to ensure you have all your essential items and documents:

- Passport and Visa (if required)
- Travel insurance documents
- Flight/train tickets and itinerary
- Accommodation reservations and contact information
- Credit/debit cards and sufficient cash in euros
- Travel adapter and chargers for electronics
- Medications and prescriptions
- Travel-sized toiletries
- Clothing suitable for the season (layers are advisable due to varying weather)

- Comfortable walking shoes

- Guidebook or maps of Aachen

- Local SIM card or international roaming plan

- Language translation apps or phrasebook

- Power bank for recharging devices on the go

- Aachen city guide or tourist information brochures

- Snacks and a reusable water bottle

- Travel lock for securing luggage

- Photocopies of important documents (passport, ID, insurance)

- Emergency contact list with important phone numbers

Currency and Banking Information

- Currency: Euro (€)

- ATMs: ATMs are widely available throughout Aachen, accepting major international credit and debit cards. Be aware of any foreign transaction fees imposed by your bank.

- Currency Exchange: You can exchange currency at banks, exchange offices, and some hotels. Rates may vary, so it's advisable to compare rates before exchanging money.

- Credit Cards: Credit cards, including Visa and MasterCard, are widely accepted in Aachen. However, it's a good idea to carry some cash for small purchases and in case you visit places that do not accept cards.

By utilizing these travel apps, following the travel checklist, and being well-informed about currency and banking matters, you'll be well-prepared for your journey to Aachen. Enjoy your travels and make the most of your time exploring this captivating city!

APPENDIX II:
German Phrases for Travelers

As you embark on your adventure in Aachen, having some basic German phrases at your disposal can enhance your travel experience and help you connect with locals. Here are useful phrases for various situations:

Basic Expressions for Travelers

1. Hello: Hallo (hah-loh)

2. Good morning: Guten Morgen (goo-ten mohr-ghen)

3. Good afternoon: Guten Tag (goo-ten tahk)

4. Good evening: Guten Abend (goo-ten ah-bent)

5. Thank you: Danke (dahn-kuh)

6. Yes: Ja (yah)

7. No: Nein (nine)

8. Please: Bitte (bih-teh)

9. Excuse me / Sorry: Entschuldigung (ent-shool-dee-goong)

10. How much is this?: Wie viel kostet das? (vee feel kohstet dahs?)

11. Where is...?: Wo ist...? (voh ist...?)

12. I don't understand: Ich verstehe nicht (ikh fer-shtay-uh nikht)

13. Can you help me?: Können Sie mir helfen? (kuh-nen zee meer hel-fen?)

14. I need a doctor: Ich brauche einen Arzt (ikh brow-khuh eye-nen ahrts)

15. I'm lost: Ich habe mich verirrt (ikh hah-buh meekh fer-eert)

Ordering Food and Drinks

16. Menu, please: Die Karte, bitte (dee kahr-teh, bih-teh)

17. Water: Wasser (vahs-ser)

18. Beer: Bier (beer)

19. Coffee: Kaffee (kah-feh)

20. Tea: Tee (teh)

21. I would like...: Ich hätte gerne... (ikh hah-teh gehr-neh...)

22. Vegetarian: Vegetarisch (veh-ge-tah-rish)

23. Spicy: Scharf (shahrf)

24. Delicious: Lecker (leh-kuhr)

25. Bill, please: Die Rechnung, bitte (dee rek-noonk, bih-teh)

Navigating Public Transportation

26. Where is the bus station?: Wo ist die Bushaltestelle? (voh ist dee boos-hahl-teh-shteh-luh?)

27. How much is a ticket to...?: Wie viel kostet eine Fahrkarte nach...? (vee feel kohstet eye-neh fahr-kahr-teh nahkh...?)

28. Train station: Bahnhof (bahnh-hof)

29. Taxi: Taxi (tahk-see)

30. How much to go to...?: Wie viel kostet die Fahrt nach...? (vee feel kohstet dee fahrt nahkh...?)

31. Left: Links (lehnks)

32. Right: Rechts (rekhts)

33. Straight ahead: Geradeaus (geh-rah-deh-ows)

34. Stop here: Hier anhalten (hee-er ahn-hahl-ten)

35. Airport: Flughafen (floog-hah-fen)

Having these German phrases at your disposal will help you navigate Aachen with greater ease and connect with the locals. Most Germans appreciate it when visitors make an effort to speak their language, even if it's just a few words. Enjoy your time in Aachen and immerse yourself in the local culture!

APPENDIX III:

Maps of Aachen, Germany

Printed in Great Britain
by Amazon

36881419R00056